Raft of Days

Praise for *Raft of Days*

There is a brilliant subtlety to this witnessing, a knowing tenderness that explores our relationships with the natural world and those we love. These poems exalt the moment and explore the geography of memory, with a spare clarity that evokes our finest lyric poets' imaginations. Everything matters in Catherine Abbey Hodges' world: temperature, math, violet, penny—she transforms the ordinary into art, into breathtaking poems that call to you again and again. This poet is a marvel. *Raft of Days* is a treasure.

—Lee Herrick, author of *Gardening Secrets of the Dead*

Because she's honed the art of looking inward and outward at the same time in *Raft of Days*, Catherine Abbey Hodges writes poems that manage to be small and also large, quiet while eventful, realistic yet reverent, both evocative and clear. She acknowledges the "dark sand and dark/ stones on a dark morning," but chooses to see the single crab shell that's "bright as a poppy." Her poetry produces more than pleasure. It is an antidote to despair.

—Susan Cohen, author of *A Different Wakeful Animal*

A unique voice is one thing; a true voice that pays close attention to the world is something else again. Put them together and you have the exceptional yet eminently accessible poems of *Raft of Days*. Catherine Abbey Hodges distills the rush of experience into clear and deeply human poems. She has an appreciation for the spiritual glowing just inside the physical world. This is an insightful yet modest poetry, a compassionate and original vision.

—Christopher Buckley, author of *Star Journal: Selected Poems*

In her second collection of poems, Catherine Abbey Hodges seeks grace in the natural geometries of light-seamed clouds and evening skies, comfort in rain and birds and humble garden flowers. Her meditations are a way of marking time and mortality—her own and that of those she loves. Sorrow is balanced alongside wonder, and the complexities of faith huddle close to the ordinary work of cooking, making lists, and keeping a steady breath. This is an authentic and beautiful book.

—Emma Trelles, author of *Tropicalia*

Also from Gunpowder Press:
The Tarnation of Faust: Poems by David Case
Mouth & Fruit: Poems by Chryss Yost
Shaping Water: Poems by Barry Spacks
Original Face: Poems by Jim Peterson
Instead of Sadness: Poems by Catherine Abbey Hodges
What Breathes Us: Santa Barbara Poets Laureate, 2005-2015
Edited by David Starkey
Burning Down Disneyland: Poems by Kurt Olsson
Unfinished City: Poems by Nan Cohen

Shoreline Voices Projects:
Buzz: Poets Respond to SWARM
Edited by Nancy Gifford and Chryss Yost
Rare Feathers: Poems on Birds & Art
Edited by Nancy Gifford, Chryss Yost, and George Yatchisin

Raft of Days

POEMS

Catherine Abbey Hodges

Gunpowder Press • Santa Barbara
2017

© 2017 Catherine Abbey Hodges

Published by Gunpowder Press
David Starkey, Editor
PO Box 60035
Santa Barbara, CA 93160-0035

Author Photo: Rob Hodges
ISBN-13: 978-0-9986458-1-0

www.gunpowderpress.com

For my sisters Anna and Mim
and my brother Russell

Acknowledgements

Gratitude to the editors of the following publications, in which a number of the poems in this book first appeared or are forthcoming, some in earlier versions or under different titles:

All the While (Finishing Line Press): "Evening at Maureen's," "Evening Prayer, Sumatra," "Fine and Fast," "On the Equator" and "The Possibilities of Blue"

The American Journal of Poetry: "Sparrows" and "Umtanum Ridge"

Askew: "Cinnamon Teal," "My Aunt's Campaign to Save an Overused Word," "Post-Election Semi-Glosa" and "To My Body with a Chest Cold"

Christian Century: "Easy"

Into the Teeth of the Wind: "Appetites" and "The Common, the Latin"

Levan Humanities Review: "Woman with Fish in Her Hair"

Miramar: "Calculus of Leaves," "Cat of the World," "One Violet in February" and "Original Hands"

"Easy" also appeared in *All the While*.

Contents

I.

Cinnamon Teal	15
San Juan Island with Lit Faces	17
On the Equator	18
One Day, Near the End of the Twentieth Century	19
Fine and Fast	20
The Summer I Turned Fifty-Two	21
Post-Election Semi-Glosa	22

II.

Still Burning	25
Flying Away: Late Spring Morning in the San Joaquin Valley, 1944	27
Standing in the Street	28
On Lewis Hill	29
Dorothy Day as a Pebble and a Perseid Meteor	30
Photo with My Siblings	31
Autumn Sunflower	32
Easy	33
Oak Tree on San Andres Street	34
Calculus of Leaves	35
What Water Remembers	36
Evening Prayer, Sumatra	37

III.

Umtanum Ridge	41
At Tina's: Meditation on Names	43
My Aunt's Campaign to Save an Overused Word	44
Woman with Fish in her Hair	45

Far Inland — 46
Penny — 47
Undomesticated Star — 48
Geographies — 49
Nocturne with Hourglass — 50
In the Heavens and in the Earth — 51
Vows — 52
No Freesias — 53
How I Trust the Hours — 54

IV.

Cat of the World — 57
To My Body with a Chest Cold — 58
A Stranger Hands Me a Memory — 59
Thrift — 60
Holding Still — 61
A Few Prayers — 62
Un-Named Sorrow — 63
Dust See Us — 64
Sparrows — 65

V.

Sixth Grade Math with Mrs. Pfeil: An Extrapolation — 69
The Common, the Latin — 70
A Pity, Say Some — 71
Appetites — 72
The Possiblities of Blue — 73
In the Photo — 74
Evening at Maureen's — 75
Off the Coast of Everywhere — 76
One Violet in February — 77

*How shall the heart be reconciled
to its feast of losses?*

—Stanley Kunitz

*The longer you look at a thing
the more it transforms.*

—Anne Michaels

I.

Cinnamon Teal

—November 2016, San Juan Island

Later of course I read
that what I'd thought
were cinnamon teal—intrepid
pair on a cold sea,
so cinnamon, so teal—
were probably not
as they haven't been identified
here for over a decade,
climate changing
as it has been,
but at the time
I was unaccountably happy
thinking that's what they were,
repeating the two words
like a chant
to the driftwood
as the tide rolled
its clicking stones to shore
and sucked them out again.

And though I got it wrong,
that hasn't kept me
from savoring the name,
its velvety mouthfeel,
just one of the things to love
about poetry,
though I'll be the first
to say I love the world even more,

by which I mean the actual
ducks and pebbles
and driftwood, cormorants
and ancient murrelets—
all parables of reproach...
the Doug firs splitting
rocks, the wintering loons
and buffleheads.
Especially I love this:
the delicate crab shell
that survived
the rough and tumble of tides
on Haro Strait
in late November
and has come to rest here
for now
on the dark sand and dark
stones on a dark morning
bright as a poppy.

San Juan Island with Lit Faces

On this island far from home,
days long past
flicker like lit faces
between trees at dusk.

What is our business
with each other
after all this time?

Do I owe them something?
Or they me?

Or is this where we meet
to share the light-shot fog,
the bread crusts we have left?

On the Equator

Fresh from netting golden carp
my child sits on wet green tiles, scrubs
his toes with an old toothbrush.

This year we live in Indonesia
where the equator seems at times to run straight
through me. This could explain the ripping,

as if I were a piece of cloth
torn quickly down my length by brisk,
business-like hands: the sudden

loud unzipping of my story about the world,
the ways we set ourselves on fire,
ourselves and one another.

The bombs and the water lilies, the ravishing
scent of cloves from the cigarette factory

across the river, my son's toes flashing
like fish caught in braids of sunlight
deep in some green pool.

One Day, Near the End of the Twentieth Century,

our mother remembered.

First, though, she needed
a vessel to hold
the scalding soup of it.

So she made a big yellow bowl,
our childhood—

peanut butter sandwiches wrapped
in waxed paper
and tucked in lunch bags,
dimes for milk,
stacks of handkerchiefs
sprinkled, layered, rolled, ironed,
dinner bell on the back porch—
some nights candles.

Only then did she recall
how her father had come to her room
all those nights
while her thrifty mother, stitching,
always stitching,
had darned and mended
every day:

no rips, no tears, only the scalding soup,
the river under the bed, beneath the floor,
flowing from the house
at the quiet edge of the canyon
all the way
here.

Fine and Fast

I don't recall the afternoon,
only the photo, now gone too.
In it I sit beside my mother
on some broad beach,
stand of dark trees
behind us. It's 1960, and sand
streams through my
loosely cupped hands
as it has ever since:

through and away
so fine and fast
just this side of the dark.

The Summer I Turned Fifty-Two

That summer when every day was another dream dead
        or the same one dead a different way and the world
rumbled on, clueless and crude, I'd sit out back past dark,

        sweat, look up through gritty haze at what stars I could find,
hope for solace or at least perspective. Even a breeze
        would have been something. An eternity of this. Then

one night something stirred in the ruined garden. I dropped
        my gaze, watched a toad rustle free of the tangle.
Its alien toes parted the grasses as it pulled itself forward,

        and I was a child again. That's all I know to tell.
The toad advanced, graceless in the murky dark
        and weirdly dear, a creature I knew once, hope to know again.

Post-Election Semi-Glosa

> *All things want to be heard,*
> *so let us listen to what they say.*
> *In the end we will hear what we are:*
> *The orchard or the road leading past.*
>   —Rainer Maria Rilke

Clock in America's pawnshop
window, hour hand a bent fork,
minute hand a toothless knife,
old apple orchard not dead yet,
still spilling apples down the road,
rug a child unrolls to pray,
burst of pigeon wings…
from these come no word,
yet all things want to be heard,
so let us listen to what they say.

I know. It's near-impossible
to hear over the shrilling
headlines and ringing silences,
over the bullhorns
and the gnashing teeth,
over the anthemic bullybombast,
yet we still have these ears, so let us
listen, hold or crack our hearts ajar.
In the end we will hear what we are:
The orchard or the road leading past.

II.

Still Burning

On the drive back to college after a weekend at home
I hit congestion on the 210 just before Pasadena,
the kind of slowing that makes you think
there's been an accident, and then I saw it ahead
just as I heard the first sirens—a single car
on the narrow left shoulder, engulfed in flames.
Drivers on both sides of the freeway were giving
the blaze a wide berth in a slow, terrible
river flowing both directions at the same time,
parting for a moment around a fiery island.
When I came up parallel two lanes away
I saw two hands pressed against the window
in the back seat, bit the back of my own hand.

Thirty years later in San Francisco I skipped out
on a late afternoon session at a conference.
It was January and windy, and I pulled my jacket
tight, thrust my hands into my pockets.
I wandered between street vendors,
fingering crocheted caps and holding hand-blown
glass beads to the light. I bought a pair of earrings,
then crossed to the Market Street Ferry
Building. There, just beyond the massive
front doors, two outsized wooden clock hands,
hour hand on top of minute hand, hung
horizontal under glass in a long, narrow frame—
the original hands, read the brass plaque,
of the Ferry Building Clock, the largest mechanical
clock in the world. Through an arched

window the setting sun stained the sky and sea.
And though of course it was the sea, what I saw
was a river, flowing two directions at once,
me two lanes away, burning still.

Flying Away: Late Spring Morning in the San Joaquin Valley, 1944

For my father's 87th birthday, I want to release 87 homing pigeons, stand with him as he was at 15 at his first job, having run on the double when he got the call to the small-town railway station where rectangular baskets of birds had just arrived from Los Angeles for the big race back over the mountains. It's a late spring morning, and my dad is puffing and sweating with his pal Jack Rider and a handful of their friends, pretending to listen to the familiar instructions, and then, on cue, as fast as he can, releasing the latches on his assigned stack of baskets.

I want to stand with him and hear the flap and mutter of 87 pigeons, blink with him and see the birds blink in the light already smothered in heat.

I want to watch the fabled chaos of takeoff and the rising, the legendary circling, higher each time, then the choreographed exit, after three full circles, from the gyre—band of dark bodies headed straight for the mountains.

I want to stand with him and watch them fade from view, 87 pigeons racing homeward.

I want to look him in the eyes and thank him, then disappear before he can ask who I am and what I have to thank him for.

Standing in the Street

Twilight, and bodies in flight:
mosquitoes, bats, the International
Space Station—the reason

we're standing in the street, me
face-to-sky, neck
at an angle I can't hold long, Rob

looking down at his phone, bringing
up his night sky app.

Three children
on one unsteady skateboard
roll slowly by, giggling, arms extended,

speaking a language I've forgotten.
I recognize their happiness, though,
and my own

in this realm of wonders—
all of us in flight.

On Lewis Hill

—after Linda Pastan

She's editing her almanac of middle things, though who can tell the middle
any time before the end? We have nothing but statistics from other lives
to go on, data twitching with anomaly.

Still, she's revising toward clarity, erasing last May's mattress fifteen feet
off the road on Lewis Hill and all but hidden by the wild mustard
and bindweed. Also the clearer view of it after the leafy

screen crisped and withered mid-summer. Crossing out
the charred springs, all that remained of weeds and mattress both
once the fire flashed through in August. And here are the blackened coils

haloed in frost, what she knew she'd see this first cold morning but didn't,
some good citizen having hauled the ruin off—though there it is
anyway in her mind's eye, bejeweled in the winter air,

and now she claims it for the almanac. Now she's erasing all the rest—all
but the indelible, absent coils shimmering with frost and first-light,
lighting the middle's next half mile.

Dorothy Day as a Pebble and a Perseid Meteor

Dorothy, I think you'd be impatient as hell
with the campaign to canonize you—all that
paperwork, for one thing, and at a time like this.
Dear God. No taser necessary—we're stunned
already, near-immobilized. Daniel Berrigan had
it right, and maybe we're ready to listen? I wonder,
Dorothy, can you see us here?
                                                  We're flat on our
backs in darkened parking lots and feel you
sharp as a pebble at the shoulder blade—you
and that crazy Merton, Ghandi, César and,
as Berrigan put it, *Christ, arranger and wrecker
of lives.* While we shift position and scan the inky
dome for the swift bright gash, you took
*the long route to the center, praxis banged out
on kitchen tables.*
                              We swing from despair to hope
and back, argue that each alpha's an omega and so
on blah blah blah, but you were *literal as ever, living
as though the truth were true.*
                                                  Hope was *a penny a copy*
and you—*honey in death's jawbone, bread and truth,
truth and bread, making the rounds,* pebble at our
shoulder blades, damned uncomfortable. Don't stop
now, Dorothy. It was your life's work to disturb—
there's your sainthood.
                                        Disturb us toward that light
where the vivid air is signed with your honor.

Photo with My Siblings

It must be the first day of school:
we've got that spit-and-polish
sheen, bangs pasted to foreheads,
shoes not yet scuffed. That garage

was so small the station wagon
barely fit inside. And unlit—it was like night
in there, so that in the photo of the four
of us lined up against the car's back window

in the open doorway, we're framed first
in darkness, then in morning sky caught
in the glass. We're old-photo grainy,
our faces indistinct, as if we haven't quite

materialized, as if who we will become
 is still working itself out, still
swimming in and out of us
in search of lodging.

Autumn Sunflower

Now that the gold's spent, finches
bring their delirious industry to the table.
The feast bobs and sways while behind the glass I study my ache
for the animal days of empty,
then full.

Easy

The jacaranda trees have had their day,
razzled their dazzle,
earned their annual oohs and ahs.
Now comes the slo-mo
mid-June fall from grace,
inexplicit purple shawl about the weathered neck,
easy on the grassy shoulders,

easy in the eye of the beholder
who sees all in a rush
that today's grace, this quiet draped mosaic,
is truer than yesterday's bright fanfare—
though neither is false,
and easy is anything but cheap.

Oak Tree on San Andres Street

I don't remember the art teacher's face
or name, details of the assignment, the season.
That's not true. California winter: branches
bare, concrete chill.

I remember the muscled trunk
against the violet afternoon, the facets
of the pencil in my fingers, edge of the sketch
pad on my thighs as I sat on pocked concrete, leaned
against the wall of Grace Lutheran Church
on San Andres Street.

I remember breathing in, breathing out,
that tree washing into me like a creek
on the rise as time backed away
for the first time.

Calculus of Leaves

This morning the frosted
margins of the tawny sycamore leaves

brought to mind your face
in the photo you sent last month

on New Year's day.
Hundreds of miles away,

there you were on the screen
of my phone, ice glittering your beard.

The photo brought you near,
then cast both of us

far ahead to when that silver
shimmer won't be ice

but years, and I may be
more distant still—or nearer—

or strangely both, a separation
not measurable in any math

we've learned yet, stern calculus
of leaves and frost, mothers and sons.

What Water Remembers

—after the headline "Study Shows Water Has Memory"

being dowsed
      being piped
            being poured

    being steam
        being fog
            being rain

      how it feels to race down a windshield

        being sleet
           being snow
              being ice

    how it feels to calve

        to melt

            to up and

                disappear

Evening Prayer, Sumatra

Ruly, wild and plural

  rinsed in slanting rain's devotion

    the call to prayer

spools out in all directions

  through the brief green dusk

meets calls from other mosques

    somewhere over flooded fields

finds me in my kitchen

  performs its one task

    O Lord

    God of hosts.

III.

Umtanum Ridge

That icy night on Umtanum Ridge
between Yakima and Ellensburg
we slowed and pulled off the highway
along with the few others on the road
after eleven o'clock to watch
the Northern Lights. Most

of the women were in heels
and long black dresses, the men
in tuxedos, members of the Yakima
Symphony on our way home
after a big night of Beethoven, all of us
shivering, teeth chattering, stunned

silent by the pulsing blue-green waves
of light. I thought of Stanley Kunitz
on the graveled roof of the red brick
apartment at the foot of Green Street,
waiting for Halley's Comet and the end
of the world, how the surface

would have felt under his small back
as he looked up into the sky and told
his dead father where to look for him.
I thought of our landlord's mother,
out for a visit from Queens, getting out
of the car one afternoon on the same ridge

where we stood under the Aurora,
the too much of it, all that openness,
her panicked dive back into the car
and refusal to come out despite her son's
assurance that it was fine, really, that she
was perfectly safe. And wasn't she

right? It's all too much, by night
or day—too big, too true. Flat on our backs
on the rooftops of our own lives, shivering,
talking to whoever we talk to when the hour's
late, it's hard to locate even ourselves, let
alone tell someone else where to look.

At Tina's: Meditation on Names

There's an angel on the wall
above the window. If I lie face up
on the floor, I see his chiseled
chin from underneath. He's still
young, in his second century if that,
nostrils flared, lips relaxed,
expression mild, bemused. (Why
is the human lying on the floor?)
The rough-hewn wings extend
three feet or so. He's Tina's nameless
angel, this is Tina's little room,
the garden through the window
hers as well.
              Tina says her mother
lived eight months past ninety-nine,
knew Dylan Thomas, told her how
he'd climb up on the table and shout
I am Dylan Thomas! This was not
too long before the poet shrugged it off—
his name—like a jacket on a warm
day, as we'll all slip off our names,
bequeath them to the living
who'll still find some use
for them.
          Meanwhile, in Tina's garden,
backlit blossoms mind the shop,
tend the breeze. They name
the afternoon *June's Last Farthing*
and engrave it on the air.

My Aunt's Campaign to Save an Overused Word

When my aunt decides to stop using
the word *great*, I can hardly say anything else
in her presence. That was a great meal, I say.
I tell her to have a great week, exclaim
over what I call a great view. I'm forever
retracting, abashed by my sluggish mind,
the blundering tongue that betrays it,
and worried, too, about great grandmothers,
the Great Lakes, already missing great blue herons
until it occurs to me that they're her point
and that once again I've overgeneralized,
a great tendency of mine.

Woman with Fish in her Hair

Morning beats with cedar waxwings,
flock of hundreds turning on a dime,
changing their almost
single mind

on the subject of where the berries
are sweetest, their flight
so synchronized
they could be minnows,

and instead of looking up into the pale
March sky I could be knee-deep
in an August pond looking down
at my rippling, transient face

silver bodies darting
through my hair.

Far Inland

From here I see the little teeth
that rim the leaf nearest my window,
the leaf that slaps the glass in the wet
breeze. Sooner or later I may tell you
this sight changed my life,
maybe how. Nuance, I get and spend
in your small bright coin, the almost-
missed, those sister electricities:
attention and luck.

Yet I concede
there's something to be said
for the obvious, the large and loud,
for rushing presence. Half-acre of August
sunflowers, rowdy with finches.
Pelican landing like some antique
pontoon biplane on the glassy face
of an evening lake far inland.

Penny

In what cupboard are the years
of spattered mirrors and strewn socks
stored now? They're somewhere,
pulsing still, the held breath
of waiting for everything to begin
when it already has. The one
thing out of place: a penny
winking up from the faded carpet
as I stand in your doorway

breathing the deepening distance.
Your great grandfather
advised your dad to keep his eyes
open for pennies on the ground.
People don't much notice them,
he said, *but if you pick them up
and keep them, one day you'll be glad.*
That moment too is still alive
somewhere, a dark-eyed boy

looking up at an old man.
I never met him but oh, you
would have astonished him,
flashing up like a new penny
through the motes. You'll be crossing
the state line about now, everything
before you and already begun. I'll keep
what can be kept, wish you gladness
for the road in the coin of every realm.

Undomesticated Star

What does my mother see
now she's unlearned
toothbrushes and the name
of my son?
Translucent wand,
ill-willed bristles at one end,
winsome stranger
perhaps a Norse prince
or long-ago tennis chum
back for a chat?

Perhaps, having unlearned
the constellations, she sees
the stars as we did before
we named them, before
we assigned them families,
thought them tamed.

Geographies

Mt. Sinabung's erupting again,
lava like crimson foil, neon rice fields,
running figures in sarongs blue, purple, orange.

There's a geography of the earth,
another of the body in response, the heart,
geography of light's bequest to the eye.

The mind has its own geography, and the spirit,
tectonic plates restless and shifting in secret
deeps or fire and ash. A matter of time,

say the experts. This afternoon I'll call my mother
over the mountains. She may or may not know
me, stranger in an orange skirt far away.

Nocturne with Hourglass

murmur in the fadeaway   vespers with teeth   sister of an early draft, spoken for

episodic badlands   some ID please   owl chapter   splinter chant

tumbledown paragraph   footfall footfall nightfall   night

third draft in tongues   nocturne with hourglass

with thimble   with photo   with fold

another name for you and you

a wider ledge of stars

an older dream

a second

sky

In the Heavens and in the Earth

—a cento from three sources

Something is in charge, an entity we loosely call "mind."

    Combine all the spices in a bowl.

O Almighty God, the supreme Governor of all things, whose power no creature is able to resist

    We have little understanding of how this neuronal choreography engenders us with a sense of being.

Drizzle the oil over the spices and mix well.

    Almighty God, who declarest thy glory and showest forth thy handiwork in the heavens and in the earth

If large portions of the world remain unseen or inaccessible to us, we must consider the meaning of the word "reality" with great care.

    Heat a skillet over medium-high heat.

O Eternal God, who alone spreadest out the heavens, and rules the raging of the sea

    Here is another way of thinking about this:

I have loved this recipe from the moment I tried it.

Vows

I could be younger   older
        better   worse
                richer   poorer

sicker   healthier—look
        I can see how this is starting
                to sound.

But it's only me
        ravished
                and tying the knot

plighting my troth
        to the world
                the word

unremitting amazement
                inscriptions on rain.

No Freesias

Don't give me delicate, she said. No
delphiniums, no lilies. No freesias
or maidenhair fern. Look at me.
Read my want: hot from the sun,

rough against me like a crookneck
squash vine or the muscled stalk
of summer's fattest sunflower. I want
heft and dirt, she said, not soil:

dirt. The only petals ours, tearing
away. Leaves the size of plates to lick
clean. Scent of tomatoes warm in their skins,

of basil, the thyme we'll trample as we
press against the shed. The only sound
the private roar of dying again and again.

How I Trust the Hours

Minding my own business, making a list
of things I trust since Galway Kinnell wrote
Trust the hours and I'm not sure I do, listing

leaves, cinnamon, some dogs, most pencils,
few pens, and suddenly I'm thinking of those
fat ballpoints we'd buy in junior high, the ones
with 6 or 8 or 12 colors. We'd choose

the color we wanted—turquoise, fuchsia,
root beer—and push down the little color-
coded catch that slid the right cartridge

into place. They lasted a week at most, those
cheap pens, and we didn't waste much sorrow
on them when they quit on us: we knew
where to get more. All the way until we lost

interest in them, we took for granted the supply.
Dear hours, if I trust you, and I'm not saying
I do, it probably goes something like that.

IV.

Cat of the World

Into the ground, your small self,
sack of bones and spent organs, strewn
now with violets

and rosemary. You who came
to us a cat of the world
with your folded ear and milky
eye, deemed us yours,

furred our couches, heard our rages,
left your nights' work on the mat. Suffered
the clumsy love of children, claimed
your places on their beds, trailed

them at a distance through childhood's
quick fade so that burying you feels like
burying a life, which of course it is.

To My Body with a Chest Cold

On each in-breath, you creak like an old house
after the sun goes down. And why not?
You've been my home for decades,

through weathers for which meteorologists
have no words. If I haven't thanked you,
forgive me—I've been so busy. Now I do,

peering through your attic windows at a landscape
so distant from the beach of my childhood
I step back, stunned.

Of all your gifts, old bean, this one's best—room to step
back, collect my self, puzzle over the fragments
till they make sense or something better.

Oh for that beach, though, garden-rough hands
smoothing lotion over sunburn, small birds
along the tideline, their tracks once they'd flown.

And though they rose and flew so long ago,
hear how, on each out-breath, a few still pipe
and rustle in the harbor of our ribs.

A Stranger Hands Me a Memory

You, tall sir, smack in the middle
of the hardware store parking lot,
looking straight up and mildly deranged
as you count (I am to learn)
geese in that high blue place…

you drop your gaze, smile at me
and say *seventy, seven sets of ten*,
and so bring back my young mother—

afternoon walks, my brother in a stroller,
the birds she'd name for us,
the counting games we'd play—
three robins, two phoebes in tuxedos.
On very lucky days, an oriole.

Thrift

I'd turned to toss my mother's
Braemar sweater, still the deep gold
of turmeric darkening in a skillet but gone
moth-lacy, into the Goodwill bag.

At the last minute I stopped, grabbed
scissors, snipped off the buttons:
mother-of-pearl from a time
of train travel and reel-to-reel.

I poured them hand to hand,
heard them click against each other
like pebbles at the edge of an incoming
tide. Hand to hand to hand.

When we were small, my sister
would shake our mother's bracelet case
when she was gone and imagine her
near—she told me this not long ago—

just out of view, opening the hall closet
or descending the stairs,
bangles sounding.

Holding Still

—in memory of Constance Rossell Hodges

What I think of first
when we hear: you and the child
on your lap—my daughter,
your granddaughter—
washed in Sumatran lake-light.

You're trimming her nails,
smiling as you curve
around her small body
and bend to reach her fingers
that one equatorial morning.

Head cocked, she's holding still—
small miracle—for you.
Today, breath caught,
we all are.

A Few Prayers

A poodle snatches an orange ball from the air,
bounds after a flock of gulls, loops back at her name.

Out past the line of waves, a pelican spies a dimple
on the sea, turns herself into a spear.

A man stops, points, his companion
turns, the two stare as a seal near shore

comes bounding through the closest swell,
hits the sand a sleek black lab.

On the pier's splintered pilings starfish clamp so tight
to what they need, the child in yellow stripes

can't pry one loose, drops to his knees, lets out a wail
while an old spaniel in a frenzy of what I'd call joy

rolls on his back in loose sand. And here's
the moon: pale fingerprint on the afternoon sky.

Un-Named Sorrow

The air sounds with doves, jasmine riots on the trellis,
and I've come undone, fallen apart six ways from Sunday.

Once I stop crying and blow my nose, I try to make some sense
of this. I ask my strange guest, *Do I know you? Have we met?*

No answer but the hum of bees, not meant for me. Who knows
how long I've been here, these creaky bones in this creaky chair.

Long enough that I don't expect an answer, and now I find
that I no longer need one. At last, overhead, an early star

chimes like a far-off bell. And another, soon a dusting, faint
but growing brighter. I can hear them tuning up. Presently,

the distant music starts, and I inhale the fragrance of time—
all that old light, come so far, washing over me.

Dust See Us

> *—from a hand-lettered billboard
> for dust abatement services*

Your shadow smells of pennies
at ten o'clock, dust at three.
At five, it's in the front seat
of the shadow of your car,
pacing you along

the stubbled berm. You're neck
and neck, you two. Now comes
the sign on Spruce just before
the bend: DUST SEE US.
Bright sisters,

worthy brothers, let us fall with our
groans, pops, marimba of knees
hitting the floor of a fellowship
hall that's a basketball court
on Thursdays. Like our

lives: multi-purpose, loud with echoes.
DUST, SEE US. And our shadows,
and this thing that's not a race.
Everything we yearn for
sifts on down to this.

Sparrows

Her memories of the children
run something like a crazy time-lapse
film, arbitrary at best. Nothing,

for instance, from their daughter's first
day of kindergarten. But from around
that time a zoom on a clay rabbit,

wet, half-fashioned, and the small
fingers giving it form. Their son's twelfth
birthday, if this film's to be believed,

went unremarked. But the curve of his
cheek a time she rose at four
to find him asleep on the couch,

video game badgering him to choose
his weapon? Immortalized, along
with the graves of two sparrows,

a tablespoon of sand on the sill
above the sink. The film's director
a famous recluse, unavailable for comment.

V.

Sixth Grade Math with Mrs. Pfeil: An Extrapolation

—in memory of Hester Pfeil

Once the sadness book is full,
no lines left to write on,
take that total and add to it
a row of magenta geraniums
in green pots. I'll wait a minute
while you catch up.

Now, multiply that number
by your best day ever—
the birthday you were given
the yellow plastic cash register,
or when you beat the tall girl
with pretty teeth
at the 50 yard dash,
or that day they all left you alone
to listen to the rain.

Take your answer and bury
a 1968 penny in it. Next, multiply
by the first phone number
you learned by heart. You're still
with me? Good. Now subtract
September and—here's the tricky
part—add back in some lost decades,
then a grassy hillside, a flock
of grey stones.

How do you suppose it can be,
class, that we'll all get the same
answer, every time?

The Common, the Latin

Insects blur and click
in the bright air,
trill beneath
nasturtium leaves.
It is time,
my love,
to fetch the bug book
and leaf through
in search of names.
And so I do, adding my murmur
(the common, the Latin)
to the general buzz
while morning pools
in my ears, hums
in my nostrils, pours
down my throat
into my lungs
and sends her
canny minions looping
through my blood
singing other names,
all of them
yours.

A Pity, Say Some

Inside this nasturtium blossom,
a fleur de lis. All buttery,
very French. Makes me want
my coffee and brioche.
Makes me want to change my life,

be an artist on Monmarte,
back day after day in every weather.
A pity, say some, in Paris for spring
or on their break from the shop.

Look! says a child *I think I know.*
There she is again, still painting
the same orange flower.

Appetites

Birdsong
tuneless and hinged
ratchets you up
from the old dream...

      thumb tacks, begonias,
red plaid skirt, heft and swoosh,
      crash of light
on April ravens

into an absolute dawn
draped with sleeping children—
love's freight
with appetites

      for tenderness,
      for answers you don't have
         or can't bear to give just yet,
      for cinnamon toast.

The Possiblities of Blue

Early May bristles with agapanthus spears,
the days dense with their stems,
their agnostic buds,
their reluctance to entertain
the possibilities of blue.

All the while
the Matilija poppies fill
and fill with sky. Lacquered bowls,
petal-thin, they tremble with the published
secret of the lemon planets they cradle.

In the Photo

they're laughing,
the woman
and the baby,
looking into each other's faces
and laughing
at a private joke
from very far away.

Evening at Maureen's

The mountains glow in late sun's pollen light.
Soon they'll go their ancient, sprawling purple.
Soon Orion will ascend
flat on his back
and make for heaven
while small bats whirl the inky air,
brush my ear on their wild errands.

Off the Coast of Everywhere

—for those I thought I'd lost

All there is
        is all this everything

this lake isle
        gorgeous burning
                raft of days

this falling sky
        kingfisher
                damaged ferry

some passengers
        some palimpsests of clouds
                and absent stars

this archipelago
        at the bright seam
                of sea and sky

        memory and dream
                where we meet now

One Violet in February

—for Peter Everwine

Home from Fresno, I wrote this poem,
then took out everything but the violet.
Later, a little rain fell back in.
There's no story here,

only the song of tires on the wet street
and me making my way toward
the unsayable, dowsing
my way with syllables,

silence, the goodness of friends.
I'm not there yet, not even sure
I'll know when I get there.
I couldn't be happier.

Author's Notes

"Post-Election Semi-Glosa"

> The *glosa* is a form from the fourteenth century Spanish court that honors the work of another poet, taking a quatrain from that poet's work as a *cabeza* and ending each of four ten-line stanzas with successive lines from the quatrain. Lines six and nine traditionally rhyme with the final line in the stanza. My poem abbreviates and makes free with the form.

"Dorothy Day as a Pebble and a Perseid Meteor"

> Dorothy Day (1897-1980) was a journalist and activist remembered for her radical commitment to social justice. Following her conversion to Catholicism, she started the Catholic Worker Movement. Daniel Berrigan, S.J. (1921-2016) was a peace activist and poet; the poem's italicized phrases are from his 1981 introduction to Day's autobiography, *The Long Loneliness*. The poem's last line owes a nod to Stephen Spender.

"Umtanum Ridge" draws details about Stanley Kunitz from the poem "Halley's Comet."

"Far Inland" is for Richard and Ginny Osborne.

"Undomesticated Star" appreciates Jack Gilbert's line "We must unlearn the constellations to see the stars" from his poem "Tear It Down."

"In the Heavens and in the Earth"

> The text of this cento comes from the following works: *The Island of Knowledge: The Limits of Science and the Search for Meaning* (Marcelo Gleiser); *The Indian Slow Cooker: 50 Healthy, Easy, Authentic Recipes* (Anupy Singla); and *The Book of Common Prayer*, 1952 edition.

"Cat of the World" is for Christopher Buckley.

"Holding Still" is for Judy, Connie, Craig, Jane and Rob.

"In the Photo" is for Susan and Ellie Hodges.

The palimpsests in "Off the Coast of Everywhere" are for Ann Marie Wagstaff.

For the gifts of time and solitude, thanks to Porterville College for a sabbatical; to Tina for weeks in her cottage and garden; and to the Helen Riaboff Whiteley Center at the University of Washington's Friday Harbor Labs and Dorland Mountain Arts Colony for residencies.

Gratitude to Melissa Martell Black, John Ridland, Paul Willis and Molly Fisk for thoughtful responses that improved these poems over the years of their writing; to Laure-Anne Bosselaar for the wisdom to which the book owes its shape; and to Christopher Buckley for his keen eye and generous friendship.

My thanks always to my family: Donna and Laurie Abbey; Russell, Anna and Mim Abbey; Clara and Mac Hodges; and Rob Hodges.

About the Poet

Catherine Abbey Hodges is the author of the poetry collection *Instead of Sadness*, selected by Dan Gerber as winner of the Barry Spacks Poetry Prize (Gunpowder Press, 2015), and the chapbook *All the While*. Her poems have appeared widely and been featured on *The Writer's Almanac* and *Verse Daily*. Hodges teaches English at Porterville College in California's San Joaquin Valley, where she was named 2017 Faculty of the Year. She co-coordinates California Poets in the Schools for Tulare County and collaborates with her husband, musician Rob Hodges.